# GREATEST FOOTBALL STARS

Published in the UK by Sweet Cherry Publishing Limited, 2024
Unit 36, Vulcan House, Vulcan Road,
Leicester LE5 3EF, United Kingdom

Unit 31, The Pottery, Bakers Point,
Pottery Road, Dún Laoghaire,
Dublin A96 EV18, Ireland

SWEET CHERRY and associated logos are trademarks and/or
registered trademarks of Sweet Cherry Publishing Limited.

2 4 6 8 10 9 7 5 3 1

ISBN: 978-1-80263-540-9

Greatest Football Stars:
Pelé

Text by Luke Paton
Illustrations by Sophie Jones

www.sweetcherrypublishing.com

Printed and bound in India

Sweet Cherry

# PELÉ

## THE UNOFFICIAL STORY

## WRITTEN BY
## LUKE PATON

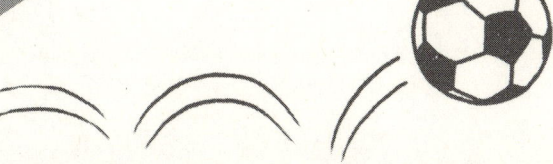

# CONTENTS

# 1
# BECOMING PELÉ

On the 23rd of October 1940, Celeste Arantes gave birth to a healthy baby boy. Her husband, Dondinho, leant over and squeezed his newborn son's thighs.

'Well, he should make a good football player,' he boasted. 'He's got the legs for it.'

Celeste protectively cuddled the baby to her chest. 'Not if I can help it!' she said. 'One football player in the family is enough!'

The new parents named their child Edson Arantes do Nascimento, but the world would come to know him better by another name: Pelé.

His father played for a Brazilian football team called Vasco da Gama. The story goes that when Pelé was three or four years old,

 Dondinho took his young son to training with him, where Pelé was

inspired by a goalkeeper called Bilé.

Pelé pretended he was the goalie, blocking make-believe shots left, right and centre. 'Good one, Bilé!' he shouted. 'Great save, Bilé!' he said. But somewhere along the way, Pelé stopped pronouncing it 'Bilé' and started saying 'Pilé'. He told his family, 'When I grow up, I want to be a goalie like Pilé.' When the family moved to Bauru in São Paulo, Brazil, the name changed again from 'Pilé' to 'Pelé'. He talked about 'Pelé' so much and so often that the kids at school started to make fun of him. They called him 'Pelé' to tease him, and Pelé got very upset.

*It's a rubbish name,* he thought. *Edson sounds so much more serious and important!*

When the other kids found out that calling him Pelé annoyed him, they called him Pelé even more! Pelé had no choice but to put up with the new name.

Pelé had to put up with a lot of things in his childhood.

Pelé's family were very poor. The house he grew up in was made of wood and had a leaky roof. Celeste was always asking Dondinho to give up his footballing dream to get a proper job and make more money.

Pelé did what he could to help. From the age of seven, he shined people's shoes to earn a little money.

What he wanted to do more than anything else was play football. He

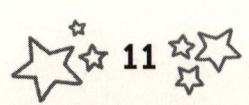 was too poor to afford an actual football, so sometimes he played with a

grapefruit or a sock stuffed with rags. Anything circle-shaped would do!

Pelé and his friends played their football games in the street, using the ends of the road as the goals. The road was full of potholes, and it was almost impossible to keep his balance, but Pelé didn't care. All that mattered was that he was playing football.

Dondinho helped him with his skills, too. 'If you ever want to be a decent player,' he said, 'you have to learn to use each foot equally.'

The pair of them trained for hours, doing drills with both feet. Then they switched to practising headers. 'Remember,' Dondinho said, 'in the middle of the forehead, eyes open, mouth closed. That's it!'

Celeste was outraged. 'Don't come  to me complaining later on when he wants to be a football player and starves to death!' she said. She thought Pelé should be a doctor or a lawyer – a job where he could earn real money.

'Don't worry, Celeste,' Dondinho

laughed. 'If he doesn't learn to use his left and right foot equally, you have nothing to worry about!'

The pivotal moment came in 1950 when Pelé was ten years old. The Brazil national football team was playing in the World Cup, which Brazil also hosted. It was only the fourth time the tournament had been played, and it was very different to the championship today.

For one thing, there were no TV

cameras. The only way for fans who weren't in the stadiums to find out what

 was happening was by listening to the radio.

The 1950 World Cup final was between Brazil and Uruguay. Whichever team won this match would be crowned champion!

Everyone in Brazil expected their team to deliver. It didn't even seem like a possibility that Uruguay might win instead.

Before the game, the mayor of Rio de Janeiro said, 'My fellow Brazilians, in a matter of minutes, you will become world champions. We kept

 our word and built this stadium. Now do your duty and win us the World Cup.'

Pelé, anticipating a historic victory, crowded around the radio with his family and friends to listen to the game.

Brazil scored just after half-time, and everything seemed to be going well. But then Uruguay equalised nineteen minutes later, then went 2-1 up with eleven minutes to go.

Suddenly, everybody listening to the radio went very quiet. The minutes ticked by ... until eventually, the final whistle blew.

Pelé couldn't believe it.

Uruguay had beaten Brazil 2-1!

Pelé started to cry ... and the tears wouldn't stop flowing. He even saw tears in his father's eyes!

He rushed upstairs and went to his parents' room. There was a crucifix on the wall, and Pelé got down on his knees to pray.

'If I had been on that field today, I swear we would have won!' he said.

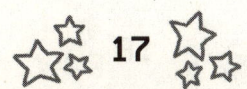

At that moment, Pelé knew he was going to be a world-famous footballer. But more importantly, he was going to get his revenge on Uruguay!

# 2
# A STAR FOR SANTOS

Pelé played for a football team called Bauru Atlético Clube Juniors when he was fourteen years old.

His coach was Waldemar de Brito, who was something of a legend in Brazilian football. He played in the 1934 World Cup and scored eighteen

goals in eighteen games for the national team.

Pelé soon found out that de Brito didn't let his teams mess around. 'When you play for me,' he said, 'you obey orders. You come to practice on time, you stay as long as I tell you to stay and when you are here you do exactly what I tell you to do.'

He didn't stand for the boys swearing or fighting or having tantrums. It was very different from the coaching they'd had before. But Pelé saw the positives to having this tough new coach.

'I will teach you all I know about the game of football,' de Brito said.

He taught Pelé how to control the ball properly with any part of his body. 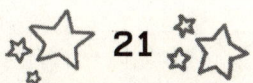 He taught him how to pass the ball to teammates using the inside or outside of his boots. He taught him how to prepare himself for what he was going to do after he got the ball. He even taught Pelé how to do a bicycle kick!

Pelé was a very special footballer, and de Brito could see it. When he left Bauru Atlético Clube to join Santos FC,

he wanted to take Pelé with him.
He went to visit Dondinho to ask for
his permission.

'Pelé should be trying out at
Santos,' de Brito said.

 'They're very good –
state champions in the
first division – and he
would have wonderful
opportunities there. I've spoken
to the top people there and they are
eager for him to come down for a trial
match.'

Dondinho was thrilled his son had a
chance to follow in his footsteps. But

 he knew there was one major issue: Celeste. Pelé's mother already hated the fact that Dondinho was a footballer. She'd hit the roof if Pelé also played the game!

De Brito and Dondinho spoke to Celeste. She said no at first, but after a lot of talking and a lot of persuasion, she finally came around.

She called her son for a chat.

'Dico,' she said. 'I don't want you to suffer in your life as we have because of football. On the other hand, you were never a good student, and I don't want you sewing boots for a living the rest of your life.'

It was official: Pelé was going to go for a try-out with Santos FC!

De Brito promised Celeste he'd look after her son when they got to Santos, a city near São Paulo. He also coached Pelé on how to make the most of his trial.

'There's no need to be nervous, Pelé,' he said. 'The thing to do is

simply forget who you're playing with.'

Pelé thought that was easier said than done.

Santos was entering a golden era.
The current squad had lots of stars
in Brazil such as Zito, Jair, Formiga,
Pagão and Pepe. Pelé wasn't sure he
could speak to these superstars let
alone play football with them!

But as soon as Pelé stepped onto
the training field, these giants of the
game treated him as an equal.

'Nervous?' Pepe asked him.

'A little,' said Pelé.

'There's nothing to be nervous
about. You're among friends.'

The Santos coach was called Lula.
He kept a close eye on Pelé during

 his trial. After all, de Brito had told him this fifteen-year-old boy was going to be the greatest football player in the world.

Lula saw that the boy had talent. There was no doubt about that. But Lula thought he was too small to play against fully grown men.

'I liked the way you played,' Lula told Pelé. 'We'll just have to wait until you're bigger and a little older, and then we'll see.'

Pelé was devastated. He was never going to make it as a professional footballer! He considered throwing it all in right there and running back home to his mother and father.

But the other players told him not to worry about it. Getting bigger was easy enough!

'We'll feed you, son – day and night!' said Pepe.

It worked. Pelé signed for the club at the end of his trial, and he was still only fifteen years old when he made his debut in September 1956.

In that first game, the team won 7-1 – and Pelé scored his first

professional goal! It was the dream debut, and Pelé felt like he'd wake up at any moment. It was all so unreal.

But things only kept getting better and better.

He carried on scoring goals for Santos, becoming their top scorer in only his second season. Before he knew it, he also made his international debut for Brazil.

His first game for Brazil was against Argentina on the 7th of July 1957 at the world-famous Maracanã Stadium. He scored on that debut, too,

and became the youngest ever scorer for Brazil! By the time people started talking about the 1958 World Cup, Pelé was a regular for both Santos and the national side. Would the rising star be part of the squad?

Pelé knew he had nowhere near the amount of experience most of the other Brazilian players had. He was only sixteen years old and didn't think he had any chance of making it to this World Cup. Maybe he'd be ready for the 1962 tournament.

Pelé was visiting his family when he heard a Brazilian radio station announce the 1958 Brazilian squad.

He listened with interest ... and perhaps a little hope.

Would any of his friends from Santos make the squad?

'Castilho ... Gilmar ...' the radio announcer said. 'Djalma Santos ... Nilton Santos ... Mazzola ...'

Then he heard his name.

'Pelé.'

He was shocked. He had to listen

to the whole thing again to make
sure he hadn't misheard.

'Pelé,' the announcer said.

He was right. It was real.

He was going to the World Cup
with Brazil!

He went to find his mother in his
daze. Was this really happening to
him?

'What's the matter with you,
Dico?' his mother said. 'Are you
coming down with

something?'

'Mama!' he said at
last. 'I've been invited

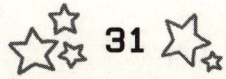

to play with Brazil at the World Cup!'

'Let me feel your forehead,' Celeste said. 'You don't look at all well!'

# 3
# WORLD CUP WONDER

*Cool, we're going to Sweden!* Pelé thought.

But it wasn't that simple.

Most fans in Brazil thought a player called Luizinho should have had a place in the squad instead of the young Pelé. Luizinho played for

a famous Brazilian team called the Corinthians.

The fans thought asking Pelé to go to the World Cup was a terrible decision, and they let the 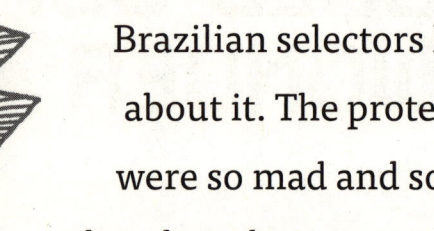 Brazilian selectors know about it. The protests were so mad and so loud that the selectors eventually set up a match between the Brazil players and the Corinthians. This gave Luizinho another chance at getting into the national team.

Pelé was playing for Brazil. But as he ran out onto the pitch, he heard

the fans booing Brazil. They were all cheering for the Corinthians, even though they were also from Brazil! It was the strangest atmosphere Pelé had ever played in.

Unfortunately for Luizinho, he didn't play well in the match, and the Corinthians went down 3-1 to Brazil. However, things were about to get very bad for Pelé.

During the game, the ball fell for him kindly, and he dribbled towards the penalty box. Then, from out of nowhere, a Corinthians player named

Ari Clemente smashed into Pelé to bring him down. He slammed into Pelé's right knee.

CRUNCH!

It felt like somebody had tried to snap his knee in two.

The physio came on the pitch to look at it. 'What do you think, Pelé? Can you go on?' he asked.

Pelé didn't want to let his team down, so he did his best to carry on playing. But as soon as he tried to walk, the pain that ripped through his leg was unbearable.

He had to be taken off.

He went straight to the changing room to receive more treatment on his knee. The doctors said it wasn't too bad, but Pelé didn't believe them. He felt like the injury was bad enough to keep him out of the squad for the World Cup.

Pelé didn't want to go to Sweden if he wouldn't be able to play. It would be heartbreaking to stay at home, but he knew it would be the right decision for the team. If Brazil was going to win this competition, they'd need all their squad fighting fit.

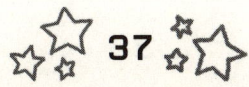

But the doctors decided Pelé was worth the risk.

They knew his knee wouldn't be healed in time for the first matches in Sweden, but they believed it would be better by the end of the group stage.

Yes! He was still going to the World Cup!

It was Pelé's first time on a plane, and his first time leaving the country. The team stayed in a luxury hotel in Gothenburg, Sweden. They became almost like a family.

They gave one another
meaningless nicknames
– Pelé was Alemão, or
'The German' – and took trips
around the city. Pelé particularly
enjoyed playing darts and visiting the
Liseberg theme park in Gothenburg.

Even though he was having the
time of his life, Pelé worried about his
knee. He had to sit on the sidelines
as Brazil won 2-0 against Austria
then tied 0-0 with England. The third
match was against the Soviet Union,
and it was one Brazil needed to win to
go through to the next stage.

Pelé trained with the team the day before the match. He played in goal at first, then moved into defence. He was testing his knee, seeing how it felt … and he thought it felt better. He moved into attack and gave it his best shot.

Vicente Feola, the coach, was watching him closely. 'It looks as though the kid is back to 100%,' he said to the doctor.

'Will you play him?' asked the team's doctor.

'Of course. I've wanted to put him in for ages.'

When Pelé played against the Soviet Union on the 15th of June 1958, he became the youngest footballer to play in a World Cup match.

When he looked at the opposition, he felt very young and small.

*They're big,* thought Pelé, *but big trees can be felled.*

He tried to remember his father's advice: 'Be confident when you step onto the pitch. Out there, everyone is equal.'

It took forty seconds of play for Brazil's Garrincha to hit the post. Pelé hit the post a minute later. A minute after that, Vavá scored and Brazil took the lead.

It was incredible! A reporter later called it 'the greatest three minutes of football ever played.'

Pelé had a couple of chances to double the lead, but he was too nervous to strike the ball properly. It was only when Vavá scored again in the 77th minute that victory was secured.

From the outside, it had been a wonderful game. But Pelé couldn't sleep that night.

He was a little disappointed in

himself. He kept playing the game over and over in his mind. What could he have done differently? Should he have scored those missed attempts on goal? He wasn't sure. All he knew was that he could have played better.

Their next match, the quarter-final, was against Wales. Brazil was the favourite to win, but Wales gave them a run for their money. It was still 0-0 at half-time, and Feola roused his men with a stirring team talk.

Pelé listened carefully to his coach

and responded first in the 66th minute.

The ball looped towards him, and he chested it down to his right foot.

 He beat a defender next, then all he to do was get past the goalkeeper. This time, Pelé didn't miss!

'Goal!' Pelé screamed in celebration.

It was his first goal in a World Cup, and the goal that took Brazil through to the semi-final!

The team celebrated in the hotel that night, with Pelé the hero of the

 hour. But they didn't go too wild. After all, they still had to beat France to be in with a chance of winning the World Cup.

The French were a good team, and they proved it when they scored an equalising goal nine minutes into the match. This was the first time the Brazilian side had conceded a goal in the entire World Cup.

But Pelé knew they had to brush it off. He picked the ball out of the Brazilian net and ran it to the halfway line. 'Let's go!' he exclaimed.

'Let's get started! Let's quit wasting time!'

His enthusiasm was just what the team needed. Didi put the Brazilians 2-1 up on thirty-nine minutes ... and then Pelé took over.

He scored one goal in the 52nd minute, another in the 64th minute and a third in the 75th minute. A hat-trick! Now not only was he the youngest footballer to play in a World Cup, but he was also the youngest person to ever score a hat-trick in one!

If anybody had doubted putting

Pelé in the squad before the tournament, they were now glad this sixteen-year-old genius was part of the squad!

The only team standing in the way of World Cup glory was the hosts, Sweden.

Brazil took it as a bad omen that Sweden also played in yellow shirts, forcing the Brazilians to change their yellow shirts to blue ones.

 'Blue will be lucky,' said the team doctor. 'It's the colour of our patron saint, Nossa Senhora de

Aparecida, and it has served previous teams well!'

Before kick-off, Pelé pictured his parents listening to the game on the radio. They'd be nervous, but they'd also be proud. He hoped they'd still be proud after the final whistle!

But things didn't start well.

The Swedes took the lead four minutes after kick-off. It was the first time Brazil had gone behind in the whole tournament!

Maybe those blue shirts were a bad sign ...

Pelé, Didi and Vavá told everybody not to panic. There was still plenty of football left to play! They just had to be focussed and confident.

They didn't need to worry for too long.

Five minutes later, Vavá equalised. He scored again just before the break, sending Brazil into the changing room 2-1 up.

'We're going to win this game and take the championship back to Brazil,' said the coach. 'The Swedes can't beat us. The only ones who can beat us now are ourselves.'

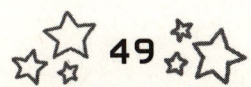

Brazil was even better in the second half. They played the kind of fluid football they were famous for.

In the 55th minute, the ball dropped towards Pelé. He controlled it with his chest as the defender approached him. Before the ball could touch the ground, Pelé flicked the ball up and over the head of the defender. Then, just as the ball was about to bounce, he slotted it home past the keeper.

*No one has seen a goal like that before!* thought Pelé.

He was right. The goal was simply magnificent. Fans still talk about it today as one of the greatest ever scored in a World Cup tournament.

But Pelé wasn't done yet. He added another goal to the scoresheet – his second and Brazil's fifth – in the last minute of normal time.

Brazil won the match 5-2.

They were World Cup champions for the first time in their history!

Pelé fell to his knees upon hearing the final whistle. He was so emotional that he

blacked out for a moment. When he came round, his teammates lifted him onto their shoulders in celebration. The scenes were crazy! The team even got to meet the king of Sweden when they were given their medals.

But Pelé only thought about his family.

*Do they know we're champions?* he wondered. There were no phones to call home, and he desperately wanted to talk to his mother and father.

'Did you see me with the Swedish king?' he said when he finally got in touch with them. 'I shook the king's hand!'

'I missed you, Dico!' his mother said.

'I missed you, too, Mama!'

# 4

# NATIONAL TREASURE

Pelé was a star.

He was loved by all in Brazil, and children wanted to be just like him when they grew up.

'Pelé! Pelé!' the crowds of fans chanted.

He was especially inspirational to

kids living in poverty, just like he did as a boy. 'I want to be Pelé!' they screamed.

For the first time in a long time, everybody in Brazil agreed on one thing: Pelé was a genius.

His name had become known all over Europe after his fantastic performance at the World Cup. Suddenly, massive clubs such as Manchester United and Juventus wanted to buy Pelé from Santos. Juventus was so desperate to sign him that they offered him shares in the car company Fiat as a bonus.

But even if Pelé had been tempted, Santos refused to sell him. Any offers for their superstar forward were immediately rejected.

People worried Santos wasn't big enough to hold onto Pelé for long, though. Everybody knew the European clubs had a lot more money and a lot more prestige than the Brazilian clubs. Besides, star players such as Vavá had already jumped

ship. Surely it was only a matter of time before Pelé followed?

The president

of Brazil, Jânio Quadros, stepped
in to finally put an end to all the
speculation.

In 1961, Quadros announced
that Pelé was now officially a 'non-
exportable national treasure.'
This meant anybody who
wanted to buy Pelé would
have to jump through all
kinds of political hoops to get
him to legally leave the country.
Pelé's 'national treasure' status
meant Santos could never sell him!

Santos was relieved – Pelé was the
main attraction of their club.

 His incredible run of goals brought the team league titles in 1958, 1960, 1961 and 1962. He'd scored 355 goals for the club, and he was still only twenty-one years old!

This incredible record came at a cost, though. Santos played an insane number of games each season. They knew people wanted to see Pelé play, so Santos played all over the world in friendlies and exhibition matches. This was on top of their regular league football. Santos wanted

everybody with enough money to buy a ticket to watch Pelé!

But Pelé was also playing football for his country. By the time the 1962 World Cup rolled around, he'd played 426 games for Santos and Brazil and scored 488 goals. It was exhausting!

The gruelling schedule caused Pelé to pick up a groin injury right before the 1962 World Cup. He didn't like to make a fuss, and he knew if he told anybody he'd be left out of the Brazil team. So, he tried to keep it as quiet as possible before the

tournament. It was easy at first.

Brazil's first match of the 1962 World Cup was against Mexico. Everybody who watched that game had no idea Pelé was hiding an injury.

He played his usual brilliant football and got his name on the scoresheet with another superb strike. Brazil won the match 2-0.

'Pelé was like no one else,' said Mexican defender Guillermo Sepúlveda. 'He was a devil!'

But afterwards, Pelé noticed his groin was hurting more than usual.

He finally went to see the doctor.

'How long has it been bothering you?' asked the doctor.

'Oh, for a while,' said Pelé.

'Can you train?'

Pelé knew he'd be dropped from the team if he didn't train. 'Oh, yes, sir!' he said.

In the next game, however, things only got worse.

Brazil were playing against Czechoslovakia. During the match, Pelé tried to shoot towards goal … and he felt something pull in his groin.

He immediately fell to the ground.

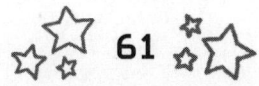

The pain was unbearable.

Teams weren't allowed to use substitutes in those days, and Pelé didn't want his side to be a man down because of him.

He tried to carry on playing, but he couldn't do much.

The game ended in a 0-0 draw.

*I don't know exactly what happened,* thought Pelé. *I'm fresh and young and I've never been injured like that.*

 After the match, the doctor checked him out again. 'You should have mentioned this a long

time ago,' he said, 'The way it is now, I doubt that you'll play in any more of the games.'

He was right. The pain was so bad that Pelé was out for the rest of the tournament. It was a disaster!

The Brazilian coaches replaced Pelé with Amarildo.

'Hey, kid, now it's up to you,' Pelé told his teammate.

It was a lot of pressure for Amarildo to take on. How could he possibly be expected to replace the greatest player in the world?! But Pelé did his best to calm him down.

'Forget about that,' he said. 'We are a team, not just one player.'

The first match Brazil played without Pelé was against Spain. Amarildo took Pelé's advice on board and scored two goals to help the team win 2-1!

Amarildo also scored in the final of the World Cup against Czechoslovakia. Brazil ended up winning 3-1, and for the second tournament in a row, they lifted the Jules Rimet trophy!

Pelé was just as thrilled as the rest of Brazil. After the celebrations were done on the pitch, he jumped in the shower fully clothed to congratulate Amarildo!

But secretly, Pelé was worried. Brazil had won the World Cup without him. Would they ever need him again?

*Am I through at the age of twenty-one?* he wondered. Is Amarildo the next Pelé?

It took two months for Pelé to recover from his groin injury. As soon as he was fit again, he was determined to prove he was still the best.

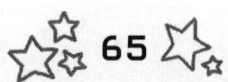

He got his chance against
Benfica in the final match of the
Intercontinental Cup.

The Intercontinental Cup was a
two-legged competition between the
South American club that won the
Copa Libertadores and the European
club that won the European Cup.
In 1962, that meant Santos faced
Benfica.

For the fans, the real treat of this tie
was seeing Pelé play against

the Portuguese striker
Eusébio. Already there
was an argument about

 who was the best player in the world – Eusébio or Pelé. This was the first time the two beloved footballers had played in the same game.

Pelé wasn't interested in that debate. 'I've never believed in a best player in the world,' he said. 'To be the best player in the world, you need to be better in every position than everyone else. And that's tricky, isn't it?'

Santos won the first leg 3-2, with Pelé scoring two goals.

Going into the second leg, Benfica was certain they could still beat Santos and win the competition. At the time, most people believed European clubs were better than South American ones. Fans of Benfica were so confident of a victory that they made banners to display around the stadium. They read: *WORLD CHAMPIONS!*

Pelé and his team saw these signs and took them as motivation to play the game of their lives!

Pelé scored his first goal fifteen minutes into the game. He doubled the lead ten minutes later with an individual piece of brilliance. Pelé glided around three helpless defenders, then blasted the ball past the goalkeeper! He completed his hat-trick in the 64th minute with another breathtaking run and finish.

Santos won the match 5-2.

Pelé later said it was 'the best game of my career' and 'a piece of footballing art I'll never forget.'

Anybody watching that day wasn't likely to forget it either.

Now the fans had no doubt: Pelé was the greatest player in the world!

# 5

# DOWN AND OUT

The problem with being a famous footballer was that the better Pelé played, the more he became a target for the opposition.

As the teams prepared for the 1966 World Cup in England, football became a very rough and tough game.

The teams from Europe were
particularly physical on the pitch,
and they knew all about Pelé.

'We have to take down Pelé,' the
teams said.

*Let's target Pelé*, they thought.

'Put three players on him!' they
decided.

Teams now thought about how to
stop Pelé by any means necessary,
instead of how best to play the match.

'It's going to be a difficult
World Cup for Brazil,'
said Pelé. 'We're going
for our third title, and

all the teams will be well prepared. But we'll do our best to win it.'

Brazilian fans certainly expected the team to come out on top. They'd won the last two World Cups. Why couldn't they make it three in a row?

Fans mobbed Pelé and the team when they arrived at their hotel in Cheshire, England. Some supporters wanted them to sign a banner that read: *THREE-TIME WORLD CHAMPIONS!* This was before Brazil had even kicked a ball in the tournament!

Pelé hoped he could deliver for the fans. His dream was to win the World Cup for the third time, then retire from international football. If he could do that, he'd achieve something no other person had achieved!

The first match of their championship was against Bulgaria. Brazil expected the competition to be tough, but this was on another level.

Dobromir Zhechev was charged with man-marking Pelé and taking him out of the game. In every area of the pitch, Zhechev tripped, kicked and fouled Pelé. Pelé got his own

 back now and then, but Zhechev did a lot of damage to Pelé throughout the game. The only time Pelé got away from him was when he had a free kick …

And that's when Pelé blasted in a stunning right-footed shot!

But when the game finished with a 2-1 Brazilian victory, Pelé was exhausted. His legs hurt from so much punishment from Zhechev!

'Football used to be more classic, something for the fans, a spectacle,' Pelé complained. 'Now teams only

play for results. Football has become ugly. Teams are playing harder!'

The coaches were also worried about how the game had changed. They were concerned that if their star attraction kept playing, he might get even more injured. 'I think every team will take care of him in the same manner,' said Vicente Feola.

Their next match was against Hungary. As Brazil had already won their first game, the coaches figured they'd easily be able to defeat

Hungary. So they left Pelé out of the team, watching from the stands.

Pelé watched the game, and hated every moment of it.

Brazil lost the match 3-1. It was the first time the team had been beaten in a World Cup match in twelve years. It was a big shock!

Feola brought Pelé back into the team for the third game in the group stage. They needed to win the game or else they faced crashing out of the competition. But they were playing Portugal, and it wasn't going to be an easy win.

 77

Portugal's João Morais shadowed Pelé for the opening of the game. He tripped and fouled him, just as Bulgaria's Zhechev had done in the previous match. And just like in the Bulgaria game, the referee rarely gave Pelé a free kick.

But Morais went well beyond what should have been allowed on a football pitch.

When Pelé got the ball on the edge of Portugal's penalty area, Morais immediately closed him down. Pelé dinked the ball to the right, away from Morais's lunging foot. Morais

brought Pelé down instead of getting anywhere near the ball.

A foul wasn't given.

Then, as Pelé tried to get back up,

 Morais flung himself at Pelé again. He missed the ball completely, and his studs crashed into Pelé's knee. CRUNCH!

Pelé went down ... and this time, he wasn't getting back up.

Fans in the stadium rose to their feet in disgust at the challenge.

Brazilian players swarmed around Pelé and the referee. Surely Morais had to be sent off for such violent conduct?

The doctors came on the field and tried to help Pelé continue. But he was in so much pain that they had to carry him off the pitch.

As for Morais, he didn't get any punishment at all. Pelé was forced to play the rest of the match on one leg, because the team wasn't allowed to use substitutes.

It was a sorry sight, and it was made even worse when Portugal won the game 3-1.

Brazil crashed out of the World Cup without even getting to the knock-out stages.

It was a disaster for Pelé, Brazil and the fans. This was not what anybody wanted.

*Football has stopped being an art, stopped drawing the crowds by its skills,* thought Pelé. *Instead, it has become an actual war.*

Pelé felt it was the worst moment in his footballing career. Not only had Brazil lost, but he'd also been injured in a way that told him football had changed forever.

*My heart isn't in playing football,* thought Pelé.

'I don't intend to play in a World Cup again because I'm not lucky in World Cups,' he later told the press. 'This is the second one I've been to where I only played two games and got injured.'

Pelé was distraught.

*What am I going to do now?* he wondered. *I could end my run there.*

# 6

# 1,000 GOALS

On the 15th of October 1969, Pelé
scored four goals against Portuguesa
de Desportos. The stunning tally took
his total number of goals for club and
country to 993.

Suddenly, fans all over the world
realised Pelé was on the brink of
scoring 1,000 goals in his career! This

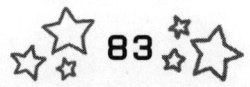

 was something only three other players had done before. It's called the milésimo.

Pelé scored two more goals in a match against Coritiba, then added another against Flamengo. By the end of October, he was standing at 996 goals. The milésimo was closer than ever!

More and more fans followed Pelé to every game. They knew he was going to reach 1,000 goals, but they didn't know when. If he could score four goals in one match, who's to say his next game wouldn't see him reach the target?

On the 12th of November 1969, Pelé got his 997th and 998th goals. His supporters could almost taste the milésimo. It was so close!

On the 14th of November, Santos played against Paraiba State XI. Pelé slotted home a penalty kick to mark his 999th goal in professional football!

*This is it!* thought the fans. *Surely nothing can stop Pelé from reaching 1,000 now!*

Santos went 3-0 up in the match against Paraiba State XI, and the supporters cheered for Pelé to hit his 1,000th goal right then and there.

But then something strange happened.

The Santos goalkeeper got injured and couldn't carry on playing ... so Pelé played in goal instead!

It's not as crazy as it sounds. Pelé had played as the goalkeeper in friendly matches before. He usually did this to save his energy for league games and have a bit of fun with the crowds.

Still, it seemed a bit odd to do it when he had the chance to score his 1,000th goal. The fans were disappointed.

The next opportunity Pelé had to score his 1,000th goal was on the 16th of November. Santos fans bundled into the stadium to watch their match against Bahia, hoping they'd bear witness to this historic event.

But another historic event was happening at the same time. On the 14th of November 1969, NASA

 launched the Apollo 12 mission. Astronauts Charles Conrad Jr, Richard Gordon Jr and Alan Bean were on their way to becoming the second crew to ever land on the Moon.

People everywhere became consumed by the question of what would happen first – Pelé scoring 1,000 goals or Apollo 12 landing on the Moon.

The astronauts weren't due to land on the lunar surface until at least the 18th. So, when Pelé played Bahia on the 16th, fans figured he'd win this strange race.

But try as he might, Pelé couldn't find the net. At one point, he hit the crossbar – only for a teammate to tap the ball home from the rebound!

Pelé started to feel the pressure. The next chance he had to score was against Vasco da Gama on the 19th of November in the Maracanã Stadium. Despite the rain, the stadium was packed with 80,000 fans desperate to see him score.

*I feel nervous,* Pelé thought before the game. *I wish the 1,000th goal was*

*over and done with! I feel
I am doomed to go for
years without scoring
another goal.*

It didn't start well.

Much like in the Bahia match, Pelé
had chances ... but none of them
went into the net.

Fans began to lose hope, until Pelé
got on the end of a Clodoaldo pass.

He was through on goal ...

And then a sliding tackle from a
defender brought him down.

Penalty!

A spot-kick wasn't the ideal way

to get to 1,000, but Pelé was going to take any chance he could to get it over and done with. He had to take it.

He placed the ball on the penalty spot and took a run-up.

But what if he missed?

*If the keeper saves it or it hits the post and rebounds, then where is the Santos team?* Pelé wondered.

He turned around … and his teammates were nowhere to be found.

Where had they gone? They should have been lined up around the penalty area!

Instead, the team was standing on the halfway line with their arms around each other.

Waiting.

Expecting.

Along with the other 80,000 people in the stadium, they were willing Pelé to score.

If Pelé wasn't nervous before, he certainly was now!

His legs were shaking.

*I cannot miss this penalty,* he thought.

He gave himself a moment to calm down, then ran towards the ball.

 92

He belted it towards the bottom right-hand corner.

The keeper guessed right and dived towards the ball.

But the shot was too strong! It struck the back of the net!

*Goal!*

Pelé grabbed the ball from the goal and clutched it to his chest.

Hundreds of fans flooded onto the football pitch.

Photographers and journalists flashed their cameras and waved their notepads in the air.

The Santos team hugged and kissed him.

Hands grabbed at Pelé and ripped his number 10 shirt from his body.

Quickly, someone put a new shirt on him. This one had the number 1,000 on the back.

His teammates lifted him on their shoulders and paraded him around the stadium. Pelé's heart was beating out of his chest and tears were falling down his cheeks.

Finally, it was over! He was eventually

substituted and allowed to head back into the changing room to collect his thoughts.

He pulled the number 1,000 shirt off his back and folded it carefully.

He'd treasure that shirt forever.

The next day, the newspapers reported two incredible events: Apollo 12 had landed on the moon at 11.45 a.m. and Pelé had scored his 1,000th goal at 6 p.m.

# MEXICO MAYHEM

Pelé's retirement from international football after the 1966 World Cup didn't last long.

He played in all six of Brazil's World Cup qualifying matches in 1969, and he scored six goals to secure his team's place in the 1970 tournament.

Pelé still wasn't sure playing in the 1970 World Cup was the right thing for him to do, though.

'I don't want to repeat what happened in England,' he said.

On the other hand, he missed playing on the world's biggest stage. If this was going to be his last chance to play in a World Cup, didn't he want to give it his best shot?

The World Cup in 1970 also promised to be different from the last World Cup.

It was in Mexico, where the temperature and the altitude are very high. A high altitude means there is less oxygen in the air, which made it harder for the players to breathe.

These conditions also made it harder for players to man-mark Pelé.

If someone was chasing one player around the pitch all day in Mexico's heat and altitude, they quickly became exhausted.

But Pelé was used to playing in these conditions. It was just like playing in Brazil.

For these reasons, Pelé decided to join the team for one last shot at World Cup glory. The one thing he didn't count on was falling out with the new coach in charge of Brazil.

João Saldanha managed Brazil during their perfect qualifying campaign, but he didn't get along well with its international star.

When Pelé suggested a different way of doing things in training, Saldanha was very unhappy.

'I'm the coach. I'm in charge!' he'd thundered in reply.

'Let's talk about it,' said Pelé.

But Saldanha never wanted to talk about it. It was his way or the highway!

Pelé worried he was making decisions that were bad for the team. He was especially worried about being asked to play as an all-out striker.

'It's not that I don't like playing there, but in my current condition, I can play deeper,' he complained. 'I've been playing deeper for fifteen years and to ask me to change how I play from one moment to the next just isn't possible.'

The conflict between the two reached bizarre new levels when Saldanha told the press Pelé was losing his eyesight.

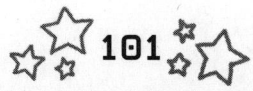

'In eighteen games Pelé has played,' Saldanha said, 'he has performed poorly in all. Particularly at night. I worry about his eyes.'

Pelé was angry. *That's nasty!* he thought.

It was only made worse when people started to believe Saldanha was telling the truth.

Saldanha campaigned to drop Pelé from the side to focus on the new players coming up in the team. Pelé was the only member of the squad who'd played in a previous World Cup, so some people questioned whether he was past his best.

The Brazilian Football Association didn't agree with Saldanha, and in the end it was Saldanha who lost his job.

He was replaced by coach Mário Zagallo two months before the tournament kicked off, and

 preparations for the World Cup started properly.

But Zagallo was still concerned about Pelé.

'What's going on, Pelé?' he asked one training session. 'You're not tackling when you're playing. You're not yourself.'

'I'm concerned for myself,' Pelé said. 'I want to be in good physical shape.'

He was worried about getting injured, just like in the 1962 and 1966 World Cups. It was affecting his game.

'Zagallo, don't pick me,' he told the coach before the tournament.

'You are like no other,' replied Zagallo. 'I will never leave you on the bench. You're going to help me win the World Cup.'

Not everybody was as confident in Pelé as Zagallo, though.

All the talk before the tournament was about how Pelé wasn't as good as he used to be.

People were saying he was too old.

People were saying his time in football was over.

Pelé had a point to prove when he went into Brazil's first game against Czechoslovakia.

# 8
# ONE MORE WORLD CUP

Pelé used the match against Czechoslovakia to unveil a new party trick.

He'd noticed that goalkeepers in Europe tended to drift away from their goal lines when the ball was in the opposition's half. Pelé thought if

a keeper ever did this while he was playing, it could provide him with the perfect opportunity to score.

During the match, Pelé got the ball ten yards into his own half. He looked up and spotted the Czechoslovakian keeper off his line. Without taking another touch, Pelé struck the ball high and long. He was going to lob the keeper from the halfway line!

The Czechoslovakian keeper was stranded and shocked.

Nobody had tried such a thing before. He pedalled

backwards, watching the ball as it floated over his head. It got closer and closer to the goal ...

Then it missed by a yard.

'Ooooooh,' the crowd cooed.

Pelé had been so close to scoring the goal of the century!

It inspired many players, including David Beckham, to try the same thing for years afterwards.

Pelé scored an hour into the Czechoslovakia game, and Brazil cruised to a 4-1 victory. This was a warning shot to the rest of the teams in the tournament. Pelé was back!

England would face Brazil next, and it was an incredibly important game.

England had won the World Cup in 1966, and Brazil had won it in 1958 and 1962. It was champion vs champion!

'It will be a game of patience,' Zagallo told his squad. 'The first one to make a mistake will pay for it, probably with the championship.'

The English defended very well, and Brazil found it hard to break through. They went in at half-time 0-0, but the team didn't panic or change their tactics. They waited for the right opportunity to strike.

Their moment came in the 59th minute.

Tostão found Pelé in the box, and the English defence prepared to block his inevitable shot. But Pelé didn't shoot. He knocked the ball to his right, where Jairzinho was waiting to blast the ball home! It was the only goal they needed to see off England.

Brazil completed their group stage with a 3-2 victory over Romania, with Pelé scoring two goals. He also helped his team ease past Peru 4-2 in the quarter-final.

But the semi-final posed a historic threat to the team.

Uruguay.

Pelé remembered his promise from when Uruguay beat Brazil 2-1 in the final of the 1950 World Cup.

 He'd sobbed after that game and said, 'If I had been on that field today, I swear we would have won!'

He'd made a promise he'd get his revenge ... and here, at last, was his chance to right the wrongs of twenty years ago.

Would fortune be on their side?

The supporters back home moaned, 'We all know how it goes against Uruguay.'

They hoped it would be different ... but football is a funny game. If the players aren't mentally prepared to win, it can all go horribly wrong despite their best preparations.

Pelé prayed before

going to bed the night before the match. 'Will everything go well tomorrow?' he asked.

The answer, at first, was no.

Uruguay got on the scoresheet first, when Luis Cubilla scored in the 19th minute.

Brazilian heads dropped.

Everybody knew what they were thinking.

The same thing had happened in 1950. Uruguay scored first then as well!

Luckily, Brazil's Clodoaldo pulled the sides level right before half-time.

But the 1-1 scoreline wasn't good enough for coach Zagallo.

'You're not even playing,' he said in the changing room at half-time. 'Now you all have to play how you know best. Not like how you were playing in the first half.'

Pelé knew he was right.

If they were going to win this match and exorcise the demons of 1950, they had to pick up the pace.

*We will win*, Pelé thought. *We just have to!*

In the second half, it was almost as if there were three Pelés on the pitch! He was everywhere and getting involved in every play.

'Now we know why they call this man the king,' said the commentator. 'Why he's the best footballer in the world.'

Pelé's display inspired Brazil to score two more goals and win the match 3-1.

They'd beaten their old rivals, but more importantly, they were going to the World Cup final!

They found out soon afterwards that their opponents in the final match were Italy.

Believe it or not, Pelé still felt nervous before he played the match. Despite all the games he'd played and the World Cups he'd already won, he couldn't get rid of the nerves.

'Dear lord, help me prepare for my last World Cup,' he prayed. 'I need your help.'

He had help from the fans, too. Their support for him and the team brought Pelé to tears. He hid his emotions from the rest of the squad because he didn't want them to think something was wrong with him. After all, they had a match to win!

Brazil naturally looked to their star player for inspiration during the game. He was the only one of them who'd done it before.

Pelé provided it in the 18th minute of the final.

Rivellino crossed the ball into the box, and Pelé leapt above the Italian defence. He seemed to hang in the air for a full second before he guided the ball into the net.

*Goal!*

Brazil was right where they wanted to be …

until the Italians equalised just before half-time.

It was 1-1 at the break, with everything to play for.

But in the second half, Brazil proved too much for Italy.

Gérson made it 2-1 in the 66th minute, and Pelé set up Jairzinho for their third goal in the 71st minute. Then the crowning glory came fifteen minutes later.

Tostão collected the ball near the Brazilian penalty area. He passed it to Brito, who knocked it to Clodoaldo.

Clodoaldo showed an individual flash of brilliance as he weaved his way around four Italian players before passing to Rivellino. Rivellino found Jairzinho with a perfectly weighted long ball, then Jairzinho squared it to Pelé. Pelé could have gone on his own run, but instead, he controlled the ball and slipped it into the path of the Brazil captain, Carlos Alberto. Alberto booted it into the bottom corner of the Italian goal!

'Delightful football!' screamed the commentator.

It was one of the best moments of any World Cup, and it put the scoreline beyond all doubt.

Brazil won the World Cup with a 4-1 victory!

Fans streamed onto the pitch after the final whistle. They gathered around Pelé and ripped off his shirt, shorts, socks and boots. He was left in nothing but his underpants!

The celebrations were long and wild.

'I'm not dead! I'm not dead! I'm not dead!' Pelé cheered in the changing room.

It was Brazil's third World Cup victory, and that meant they got to keep the Jules Rimet trophy forever. From then on, a new trophy was used at the end of a World Cup tournament.

*This is the best moment of my life,* Pelé thought.

It was the perfect way to finish his incredible career with Brazil.

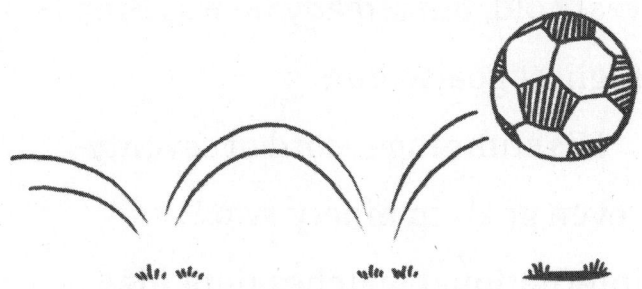

# 9
# INTO THE COSMOS

Pelé played his final game for Brazil in July 1971. He was only thirty years old, but already he was Brazil's highest goalscorer.

His stunning record of seventy-seven goals in ninety-two international matches remained

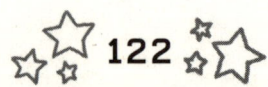

the best for more than fifty years.
Neymar finally broke the record in
September 2023, but it took him 125
matches to do it!

Pelé's last game for Santos came
in October 1974. He'd played for the
club for nineteen seasons and scored
643 league goals for them. This was
another record that lasted almost
fifty years – until Lionel Messi broke
it for Barcelona in 2020.

But Pelé wasn't done with
football.

In 1974, he signed to
play for the New York

Cosmos for three years. He had a lot of other options, but Pelé hoped to make football more popular in the United States.

It probably didn't hurt that the Cosmos paid him $7 million! That astronomical fee made Pelé the highest-paid athlete on the planet.

The fans didn't care about the money, though. Before Pelé arrived in  America, football wasn't respected as a sport. However, after the crowds saw him play, thousands of

people found a new appreciation for the beautiful game.

Pelé slotted into the Cosmos team perfectly, scoring sixty-six goals in 111 matches. Everywhere the Cosmos played, fans sold out stadiums and cheered his name. Pelé repaid their love by leading the team to two North American Soccer League titles, a Soccer Bowl and an Atlantic Coast Conference Championship.

The final match of his career arrived in October 1977. It was an exhibition game between the Cosmos and Santos – the only two professional clubs he'd ever played for. Among the 75,000 people watching were famous faces such as the boxer Muhammad Ali and England footballing legend, Bobby Moore.

Pelé played the first half with the Cosmos, then switched sides to Santos in the second half. The highlight of the game came when Pelé drilled a free kick home from thirty yards. It was his 1,281st goal, and the last official one of his incredible career.

After the match, Pelé did a lap of honour around the field and cried his eyes out. A small ceremony was held where Pelé got to speak to his thousands of fans watching in the stadium and around the world.

'Love is more important than what we can take in life,' he said after thanking everybody for watching. 'Everything passes. Please say with me, three times: Love! Love! Love!'

The crowd roared back, 'Love! Love! Love!'

Pelé cried again. It was the greatest day of his life.

He managed to say just one more thing: 'Thank you very much.'

Pelé passed away on the 29th of December 2022 at the age of eighty-two. The world of football mourned him. But Pelé will live on. His amazing achievements and his even more amazing skills continue to inspire each new generation of football players and fans.

'Pelé is the idol,' he once said. 'Pelé doesn't die. Pelé will never die. Pelé is going to go on forever.'